MAGIC WITH **MILLETS** FOR THE SOUL - A POTFUL MEAL

AN AROMATIC MEAL WITH QUICK AND EASY COOKING TECHNIQUES FOR YOUR SOUL. A STEP TOWARDS WELLNESS, HEALTH AND SUPERIOR ~ YOU!

ANINDITA MUKHOPADHYAY

Made with ❤ on the Notion Press Platform
www.notionpress.com

*Good food being an epicentre in our family a special mention to my **Baba** (Shri. Nripendranath Chakraborty) and **Maa** (Smt. Aparajita Chakraborty) who have influenced my cooking style in a very significant manner.*

Baba has a tremendous sense of taste and appreciation of good food. We have seen him being an occasional cook in our growing-up days experimenting and blending the spices to enhance the flavour of the dish.

Maa comes with her cooking skills to complement the taste buds of Baba and all of us. She is very swift in cooking and trying out new things which are quick, palatable and tasty.

Dedication of this cookbook to my Baba and Maa is a very humble gratified respect to them.

Contents

Preface

Food plays an extremely important role in today's superfast world to maintain good health and wellness. While we work on the fitness through physical exercise an rightful plate of meal is essential to complement.

My journey to explore different recipes starts with my strong taste buds which needs palatable variety in the daily meal. In this quest to do so the experiment starts to explore food which can be health friendly as well as satisfying to the soul.

A heartful meal always makes a person happy and content to take the challenges of the busy world. It's the primary fuel to our existence and wellness.

Prologue

Millets is considered as one of the super grains due to its dietary fibre values which helps in improving health and wellness for the individual. This is absolutely gluten-free, with micro-nutrients which is good for overall health and fitness.

All the recipes in the book are curated to acknowledge the taste buds keeping in moderation the health, wellness and fitness.

A special attention is given to each and every choice of ingredients so that it can be served as a wholesome meal in a busy day. Dishes are presented with a mindful thought to include protein, calcium, iron, minerals, herbs which helps also for a healthy gut and improve the cleanse mechanism for body.

These are easy, quick and simple to make with basic available kitchen essentials. All the recipes can be served in breakfast, lunch, dinner or as a quick snack for a hungry and happy stomach.

Assorted side dishes add to the plate which will make your meal palatable and enjoyable every time.

*Magic Spice Mix is a purely aromatic blend of spices carefully selected. It is the *star* which adds the special touch to each and every dish making it special!!!*

CHAPTER ONE

BASIC KITCHEN ESSENTIALS WITH BENEFITS!

Millets - *(Foxtail Millet, Little Millet, Kodo Millet or Barnyard Millet) - helps to control blood sugar, aids in weight management.*

Curry Leaves - *It is a powerful anti-oxidant and are known to offer a host of healing health benefits.*

Coriander Leaves - *It is bone friendly and works as an energy booster.*

Mint Leaves - *Improves digestions and promotes respiratory health and supports the overall health.*

Mustard Seeds - *Rich in omega 3 fatty acids which supports in improved health.*

Jeera Seeds - *It is effectively used for treating indigestion. It is rich in iron and also acts as a natural blood purifier.*

Lemon - *Lemon improves the natural glow of the skin and is loaded with vitamin C.*

Methi (Fenugreek) seeds / Methi Leaves - *Fenugreek is a full of several minerals, vitamins and polynutrients. It improves the bowel movements and helps in relieving constipation.*

Ajwain (Carom seeds) / Ajwain Leaves - *It helps in healing infections and promotes digestion.*

Lentils - *Lentils are superfood and serves as a complete source of protein.*

Vegetables - *They play tremendous role in maintaining vibrant health. it covers the complete range of vitamins which are essential for overall health.*

Asafoetida (Hing) - *Hing is a good source of potassium. It has lots of therapeutic usages and improves your overall wellbeing.*

Turmeric Powder - *It is a natural antiseptic and brings in natural golden glow to the skin.*

Ginger - *It is packed with bioactive nutrients and one of the healthiest spices used in the kitchen to promote good health.*

Garlic - *It helps to treat some of the common ailments and acts as a powerful antibiotic.*

Green Chillies - *Boosts metabolism. it is also good source of vitamins, potassium and manganese.*

Curd - *It is probiotic food substance that contains and supports the growth of beneficial bacteria in our body.*

Ghee - *Boosts immunity, helps in glowing skin and improved vision.*

Jaggery, Gud - *It's an instant body cooler and triggers energy levels.*

CHAPTER TWO

How to make Pre-cooked or Plain Millets?

Ingredients

- Millets (Foxtail Millet, Little Millet, Kodo Millet or Barnyard Millet) - wash the millets thoroughly 2-3 times to remove all the dust from the grains.
- 1 cup millets
- 2 cups luke warm water
- ½ teaspoon salt

Procedure

<u>In a pan:</u>

- Take a deep bottom pan, add the millets, water and salt together and let it boil for 8-9 minutes, in medium heat.
- Cover the pan with a lid and cook in low heat for another 3-4 minutes till the water is completely soaked.
- Switch-off the heat and let it cool for 3-4 minutes and then check if the millets are done.
- Put them in a plate and spread it so that it is fluffy and dry to be used.
- Pre-cooked millets are ready.

In a pressure cooker:

- Add the millets, water and salt in the pressure cooker and let it cook till a single whistle.
- Allow the cooker to cool down.
- Put them in a plate and spread it so that it is fluffy and dry to be used.
- Pre-cooked millets are ready.

Serve these plain simple cooked millets hot with a table spoon of desi ghee or butter along with regular Vegetable curry, Daal, Curd and Salad for a happy meal!

**** Pre-cooked millets can be kept in a box and stored in refrigerator for 2-3 days for quick use ****

Plain Cooked Millets

CHAPTER THREE

Magic Spice Mix

It's a blend of aromatic ingredients which can be used to enhance the day-to-day cooking flavour!

Ingredients

- Green Cardamom – 6 pieces
- Black Cardamom – 4 pieces
- Dalchini (Cinnamon) – 10 gms
- Javitri (Mace) – 20 gms
- Star Anise – 2 pieces
- Jeera (Cumin Seeds) – 1 tablespoon
- Dhania (Coriander Seeds) – 1 tablespoon
- Sauf (Fennel Seeds) – 2 tablespoons
- Black Pepper – 15-20 pieces
- Shah Jeera - 1 tablespoon
- Lavang (Cloves) – 10-12 pieces
- Whole Red Chilli – 3 pieces
- Tej Patta – 4 leaves
- Til/Seasame Seeds – 2 tablespoons
- Ajwain (Carom Seeds) - ½ tablespoon
- Radhuni (Wild Celery seeds) – ½ tablespoon
- Stone Flower / Dhagad Phool - 4 to 5 flakes
- Salt – 1 tablespoon

Procedure

- Take a thick bottom pan, add all the ingredients and dry roast them in a low heat for 15-20 minutes till you sense the roasted aroma. All the ingredients need continuous stir so that they don't burn.
- Let them cool.
- Coarse grind them in a blender.
- Store in a container and use when required.

**** All the ingredients are used in a very balanced proportion. Along with enhancing the taste of the dishes it also supports the digestive system of the individual. ****

CHAPTER FOUR

Mixed Vegetable Millets Khichdi

A tasty palate for a happy stomach!!!

Ingredients

- Millets – ½ cup, soak it for 10 minutes
- Splitted Green Moong Dal – ½ Cup, soak it for 10 minutes
- Magic Spice Mix – ½ tablespoon (Recipe #3)
- Ghee / Oil – 1 tablespoon
- Mix Vegetables diced – 1 Cup (Potato, Beans, Green peas, Carrot, Pumpkin, Cauliflower, Brinjal etc.)
- Jeera (Cumin Seeds) – ½ tablespoon
- Tomato – 1 diced
- Green Chillies - 2 slitted
- Water - 2 and ½ cup warm water
- Salt – ½ tablespoon or as per taste

Procedure

- Put the pressure cooker on medium heat, add ghee/oil. Add Jeera, slitted green chillies, mix vegetables, tomato and saute for 2-3 minutes.
- Add the millets and the green moong dal. Sauté for another 2-3 minutes. Add Salt and Magic Spice Mix. Add water and close the lid. Allow to cook till 2-3 whistles.
- Allow the pressure cooker to cool down.
- Serve hot with any of the side dishes. (Recipe #18)

CHAPTER FIVE

Tomato Millets

A quick evening snack or a morning breakfast!!!

Ingredients

- Millets – 1 cup, pre-cooked
- Tomatoes – ½ cup diced
- Curry Leaves – 6-8 leaves
- Rai (Mustard Seeds) – ½ tablespoon
- Green Chillies– 2 slitted
- Garlic – 2-3 cloves crushed
- Ghee / Oil – 1 tablespoon
- Turmeric powder – ½ tablespoon
- Salt – ½ tablespoon or as per taste

Procedure

- Take a Kadhai or a Pan and put it on medium heat. Add Ghee/oil and let it heat. Add mustard seeds, curry leaves, slitted green chillies and crushed garlic. Add the tomatoes, salt and turmeric power. Make the heat to low and allow the tomatoes to get cooked by stirring it once in a while. Add the pre-cooked millets and slowly mix them well with the cooked tomatoes. Sauté for 3-4 minutes. Switch off the heat and cover the pan for 1-2 minutes before serving.
- Serve hot with any of the side dishes. (Recipe #18)

COCONUT MILLETS

Quick, Quick, Quick - a mid -day meal!!!

Ingredients

- Millets – 1 Cup, pre-cooked
- Grated fresh coconut – ½ Cup
- Coriander Leaves – 1 tablespoon
- Curry Leaves - 8 to 10
- Rai (Mustard Seeds) – ½ tablespoon
- Green Chillies– 2 slitted
- Ghee / Oil – 1 tablespoon
- Salt – ½ tablespoon or as per taste

Procedure

- Take a Kadhai or a Pan and put it on medium heat. Add Ghee/oil and let it heat. Add mustard seeds, slitted green chillies and grated coconut. Add salt to taste. Sauté for 3-4 minutes. Add the pre-cooked millets and slowly mix them well. Add the coriander leaves and mix them well. Switch off the heat and cover the pan for 1-2 minutes before serving.
- Serve hot with any of the side dishes. (Recipe #18)

CHAPTER SEVEN

MULTI-HERBS FLAVOURED MILLETS

Aromatic delight!!!

Ingredients

* Millets – 1 Cup, pre-cooked
* Chopped Mint leaves – 1 tablespoon
* Chopped Coriander Leaves – 1 tablespoon
* Chopped Ajwain Leaves – 1 tablespoon (optional)
* Garlic Cloves - 5 to 6 crushed
* Onions – ½ cup chopped
* Green Chillies– 2 slitted
* Ghee / Oil – 1 tablespoon
* Salt – ½ tablespoon or as per taste

Procedure

* Take a Kadhai or a Pan and put it on medium heat. Add Ghee/oil and let it heat. Add crushed garlic, onions, slitted green chillies. Sauté for 3-4 minutes till the onions are translucent. Add the chopped coriander, mint leaves and stir for around a minute. Add salt to taste. Add the pre-cooked millets and slowly mix them well and stir them for 2-3 minutes. Switch off the heat and cover the pan for 1-2 minutes before serving.
* Serve hot with any of the side dishes. (Recipe #18)

CHAPTER EIGHT

MILLETS PULAO

Vegetables and spices which are high in dietary fibre and improves digestion!!!

Ingredients

- Millets – 1 Cup, pre-cooked
- Chopped Vegetables – 1 Cup (cauliflower, carrot, green peas, french beans)
- Chopped Coriander Leaves – 1 tablespoon
- Garlic Cloves - 5 to 6 crushed
- Green Chillies– 2 slitted
- Onions - ½ cup chopped
- Shah Jeera or Plain Jeera – ½ tablespoon
- Magic Spice Mix - 1 tablespoon
- Ghee / Oil – 1 tablespoon
- Salt – ½ tablespoon or as per taste

Procedure

- Take a Kadhai or a Pan and put it on medium heat. Add Ghee/oil and let it heat. Add Shah Jeera, crushed garlic, onions, slitted green chillies. Sauté for 3-4 minutes till the onions are translucent. Add the chopped vegetables, salt to taste, Magic Spice Mix and stir for 3-4 minutes till the vegetables are tender. Add the pre-cooked millets and slowly mix them well and stir them for 2-3 minutes. Add the coriander leaves. Switch off the heat and cover the pan for 1-2 minutes before serving.
- Serve hot with any of the side dishes. (Recipe #18)

CHAPTER NINE

SAUTÉED MILLETS

Plain sautéed millets to go with any of your curries!!!

Ingredients

- Millets – 1 Cup, pre-cooked
- Jeera (Cumin Seeds) – ½ tablespoon
- Methi (Fenugreek Seeds) – ¼ tablespoon
- Hing (Asafoetida) - ¼ tablespoon
- Chopped Coriander – 1 tablespoon
- Ghee / Oil – 1 tablespoon
- Salt – ½ tablespoon or as per taste

Procedure

- Take a Kadhai or a Pan and put it on medium heat. Add Ghee/oil and let it heat. Add Jeera and Methi seeds, let it splutter. Add the hing and salt to taste. Now add pre-cooked millets and slowly mix them well and stir them for 2-3 minutes. Add the coriander leaves. Switch off the heat and cover the pan for 1-2 minutes before serving.
- Serve hot with any of the side dishes. (Recipe #18)

Sautéed Millets

CHAPTER TEN

Green Peas Millets

Enjoy the goodness of fresh green peas!!!

Ingredients

- Millets – 1 Cup, pre-cooked
- Jeera (Cumin Seeds) – ½ tablespoon
- Garlic Cloves - 5 to 6 crushed
- Green Chillies– 2 slitted
- Chopped Coriander and Mint leaves – 1 tablespoon
- Fresh (frozen) green peas – ½ cup
- Magic Spice Mix - ½ tablespoon
- Ghee / Oil – 1 tablespoon
- Salt – ½ tablespoon or as per taste

Procedure

- Take a Kadhai or a Pan and put it on medium heat. Add Ghee/oil and let it heat. Add Jeera, crushed garlic and green chillies, let it splutter. Add fresh peas and salt to taste. Stir for another 1-2 minutes. Add pre-cooked millets and slowly mix them well and stir them for 2-3 minutes. Add the Magic Spice Mix, coriander-mint leaves and mix well. Switch off the heat and cover the pan for 1-2 minutes before serving.
- Serve hot with any of the side dishes. (Recipe #18)

POTATO-CAULIFLOWER MASALA MILLETS

Cauliflower is low-carb and rich in fibre, supports natural detox!!!

Ingredients

- Millets – 1 Cup, pre-cooked
- Jeera (Cumin Seeds) – ½ tablespoon
- Green fresh mix - Coarse grind garlic cloves (5 to 6) + green chillies (2) + ginger (1 inch)
- Chopped Coriander – 1 tablespoon
- Grated fresh coconut – 1 tablespoon
- Cauliflower - Diced, ½ cup
- Potato - Diced, ½ cup
- Fresh (frozen) green peas – ½ cup (optional)
- Magic Spice Mix - ½ tablespoon
- Ghee / Oil – 1½ tablespoon
- Salt – ½ tablespoon or as per taste

Procedure

- Take a Kadhai or a Pan and put it on medium heat. Add Ghee/oil and let it heat. Add Jeera, diced cauliflower, diced potato and green peas. Stir for another 2-3 minutes. Add the green fresh mix and stir again. Lower the heat and allow the vegetables to become tender. It may take 5-8 minutes. If required add little water. Once the vegetables are done add pre-cooked millets and slowly mix them well and stir them for 2-3 minutes. Add the Magic Spice Mix, coriander leaves and mix well. Add the grated fresh coconut. Switch off the heat and cover the pan for 1-2

minutes before serving.
- Serve hot with any of the side dishes. (Recipe #18)

Tomato Millets

CHAPTER TWELVE

CAPSICUM AND TOMATO MILLETS

Capsicum has variety of nutrients and are rich in vitamins C and B6. Tomato is full of anti-oxidants. Helps to improve the gut health!!!

Ingredients

- Millets – 1 Cup, pre-cooked
- Jeera (Cumin Seeds) – ½ tablespoon
- Capsicum medium - 1 - diced
- Tomato medium - 1 - diced
- Chopped Coriander – 1 tablespoon
- Garlic cloves – 5 to 6 crushed
- Curry Leaves - 8 to 10
- Green Chillies– 2 slitted
- Ghee / Oil – 1½ tablespoon
- Salt – ½ tablespoon or as per taste
- Turmeric powder – ½ tablespoon

Procedure

- Take a Kadhai or a Pan and put it on medium heat. Add Ghee/oil and let it heat. Add Jeera, crushed garlic, curry leaves, green chillies, diced capsicum and tomato. Stir for 2-3 minutes and add salt to taste and turmeric powder. Lower the heat and allow the vegetables to become tender. It may take 2-3 minutes. Add pre-cooked millets and slowly mix them well and stir them for 2-3 minutes. Add coriander leaves and mix well. Switch off the heat and cover the pan for 1-2 minutes before serving.
- Serve hot with any of the side dishes. (Recipe #18)

Lemon Millets

CHAPTER THIRTEEN

Lemon Millets

Lemon is rich source of vitamin C and broadly supports our immune system !!!

Ingredients

- Millets – 1 Cup, pre-cooked
- Jeera (Cumin Seeds) – ½ tablespoon
- Dhania (Coriander Seeds) – ½ tablespoon
- Rai (Mustard Seeds) – ½ tablespoon
- Roasted Peanuts - 1 tablespoon
- Roasted Chana - 1 tablespoon
- Chopped Coriander – 1 tablespoon
- Curry Leaves - 8 to 10
- Green Chillies– 2 slitted
- Fresh Lemon - 1 medium, cut into halve to squeeze the juice **or** 1½ tablespoon lime juice.
- Ghee / Oil – 1½ tablespoon
- Salt – ½ tablespoon or as per taste

Procedure

- Add lime juice to the pre-cooked millets and mix well. Keep it aside. Take a Kadhai or a Pan and put it on medium heat. Add Ghee/oil and let it heat. Add Jeera, dhania seeds, rai, curry leaves, green chillies, roasted peanuts and roasted chana. Stir for 2-3 minutes and add salt to taste. Slowly add the pre-cooked millets and mix them well. Stir them for 2-3 minutes. Add coriander leaves and mix well. Switch off the heat and cover the pan for 1-2 minutes before serving.
- Serve hot with any of the side dishes. (Recipe #18)

Peanut and Sesame Millets

CHAPTER FOURTEEN

PEANUT AND SESAME MILLETS

Peanuts and Sesame are a very good source of potassium. It is also a very good antioxidant which has a protective effect towards a healthy body!!!

Ingredients

- Millets – 1 Cup, pre-cooked
- Jeera (Cumin Seeds) – ½ tablespoon
- Roasted Peanuts - coarsely grinded - 1 tablespoon
- Roasted Sesame - coarsely grinded - 1 tablespoon
- Chopped Coriander – 1 tablespoon
- Boiled Potato diced - ½ cup
- Green Chillies– 2 slitted
- Turmeric powder - ½ tablespoon
- Ghee / Oil – 1 tablespoon
- Salt – ½ tablespoon or as per taste

Procedure

- Take a Kadhai or a Pan and put it on medium heat. Add Ghee/oil and let it heat. Add Jeera, green chillies, boiled potatoes and turmeric powder. Stir for 2-3 minutes and add salt to taste. Slowly add the pre-cooked millets and mix them well. Stir them for 2-3 minutes. Add the coarsely grinded peanuts and sesame seeds. Mix them well together and stir for 2-3 minutes. Add coriander leaves and mix well. Switch off the heat and cover the pan for 1-2 minutes before serving.
- Serve hot with any of the side dishes. (Recipe #18)

CHAPTER FIFTEEN

RAW MANGO MILLETS

Raw mangoes are a potent source of vitamin C. It has a very good fibre content which aids to improved digestion for good health!!!

Ingredients

- Millets – 1 Cup, pre-cooked
- Jeera (Cumin Seeds) – ½ tablespoon
- Methi (Fenugreek Seeds) – ½ tablespoon
- Hing (Asafoetida) – ½ tablespoon
- Curry leaves - 8 to 10
- Raw Mango - diced - ½ cup
- Chopped Coriander – 1 tablespoon
- Green Chillies– 2 slitted
- Turmeric powder - ½ tablespoon
- Ghee / Oil – 1 tablespoon
- Salt – ½ tablespoon or as per taste

Procedure

- Take a Kadhai or a Pan and put it on medium heat. Add Ghee/oil and let it heat. Add Jeera, green chillies, methi, hing, curry leaves, turmeric powder and the raw mangoes. Stir for 2-3 minutes and add salt to taste. Slowly add the pre-cooked millets and mix them well. Stir them for 2-3 minutes. Add coriander leaves and mix well. Switch off the heat and cover the pan for 1-2 minutes before serving.
- Serve hot with any of the side dishes. (Recipe #18)

CHAPTER SIXTEEN

MASALA MILLETS WITH SAMBHAR POWDER

A wholesome nutritious meal with lots of vegetables, lentils which is rich in protein and vitamins!!!

Ingredients

- Millets – 1 Cup, soaked for 5 minutes
- Toor dal (Pigeon peas) or any dal of your choice - ½ cup soaked for 5 minutes
- Tamarind Paste - 1 tablespoon (optional)
- Sambhar Powder - 1½ tablespoon (Available in any grocery store)
- Turmeric powder - ½ tablespoon
- Diced Vegetables - (carrot, drum-sticks, brinjal, pumpkin, bottle gourd, bean etc.) - 1 cup
- Small onions - 8 to 10
- Jeera (Cumin Seeds) – ½ tablespoon
- Curry leaves - 8 to 10
- Tomato - diced - ½ cup
- Chopped Coriander – 1 tablespoon
- Green Chillies– 2 slitted
- Ghee / Oil – 2 tablespoons
- Luke warm water - 3½ cups
- Salt – ½ tablespoon or as per taste

Procedure

- Take a pressure cooker. Add ghee and let it heat. Add Jeera, small onions and stir for 10-15 seconds in medium heat. Add green chillies, tomato, diced vegetables, curry leaves, turmeric powder and stir for another 2-3 minutes. Add the tamarind paste, salt to taste and mix well. Add the Sambhar powder and stir for another 1-2 minutes. Add the soaked Millets and Toor dal. Stir for 2-3 minutes. Add luke warm water and close the pressure cooker lid. Cook till 3 whistles.
- Allow the cooker to cool. Open the lid and add ½ tablespoon ghee and chopped coriander leaves.
- Serve hot with any of the side dishes. (Recipe #18)

Diced Vegetables for Sambhar Millets

CHAPTER SEVENTEEN

MILLETS PANCAKES

A healthy start of the day with goodness of protein and vitamins!!!

Ingredients

- Millets – 1 Cup, soaked for 3-4 hours
- Mixed dal (Splitted Green Moong + Masoor + Toor + Udad dal) - 1 cup, soaked for 3-4 hours
- Turmeric powder - ½ tablespoon
- Ginger Crushed - 1 inch
- Garlic Crushed - 8 to 10 cloves
- Green Chillies – 2
- Jeera (Cumin Seeds) – ½ tablespoon
- Chopped Coriander – 1 tablespoon
- Ghee / Oil – 2 tablespoons
- Water - 1 cup
- Salt – ½ tablespoon or as per taste

Procedure

- Grind the soaked millets, mixed dal, ginger, garlic, green chillies and salt to make a smooth batter. Take out the batter in a bowl. Add Jeera and coriander leaves in the batter.
- Take a non-stick pan and let it heat. Brush it with ghee. Add 2 scoops of batter. Spread it to make a 4-5 inch pancake. Cook on both side on high to medium heat till golden colour.
- Serve hot with any of the side dishes. (Recipe #18)

Millets Pancakes

Side Dishes with Millets

Assorted Potato Raita - *Take diced boiled potatoes ½ cup, add ½ cup curd, ½ teaspoon Magic Spice Mix, ½ teaspoon black pepper powder, chopped coriander leaves and salt to taste. Mix well and add seasoning.*

Assorted Fruits Raita - *Take assorted diced fruits of your choice ½ cup, add ½ cup curd, ½ teaspoon Magic Spice Mix, ½ teaspoon black pepper powder, chopped coriander leaves and salt to taste. Mix well and add seasoning.*

Flavoured Thickened Curd - *Take 1 cup thick curd add ½ teaspoon Magic Spice Mix, chopped mint leaves and salt to taste. Mix well and add seasoning.*

Sprouts Raita - *Take sprouts ½ cup, add ½ cup curd, ½ teaspoon Magic Spice Mix, ½ teaspoon black pepper powder, chopped coriander leaves and salt to taste. Mix well and add seasoning. Adding curd is optional.*

Cucumber and Carrot Raita - *Take grated cucumber and carrot ½ cup, add ½ cup curd, ½ teaspoon Magic Spice Mix, ½ teaspoon black pepper powder, chopped coriander leaves and salt to taste. Mix well and add seasoning.*

Tomato Delight - *Take a kadhai and add 1 tablespoon of ghee/oil, let it heat till medium hot. Add Jeera, 1-2 crushed garlic, 1 cup tomato or tomato puree, ½ teaspoon Magic Spice Mix, ½ teaspoon turmeric powder, 1 chopped green chili, and salt to taste. Stir for 2-3 minutes. Allow the tomato to become tender. Add chopped coriander leaves and mix well. Remove from heat and serve.*

Green Chutney - *Take handful of fresh coriander leaves, mint leaves, one small diced tomato, 2-3 cloves of garlic, ½ teaspoon Jeera, 1 green chilly, salt to taste. Coarse grind them all together. A freshly prepared chutney is ready to be served. Mix well and add seasoning (optional)*

Coconut Chutney - *Take handful of fresh coriander leaves, mint leaves, grated fresh coconut 3 tablespoon, 2-3 cloves of garlic, ½ teaspoon Jeera, 1 tablespoon lime juice or fresh curd, 1 green chilly, salt to taste. Grind them well to make a smooth paste. Mix well and add seasoning.*

Plain Boiled Dal (Any Lentil of your choice) - *Take 1 cup of any boiled dal, add fresh chopped coriander leaves, 1 chopped green chili and salt to taste. Mix well and add seasoning.*

***** Seasoning ***** - *Take 1 teaspoon of ghee/oil and heat it. Remove from heat and add ¼ Jeera, ¼Mustard Seeds, ¼Hing. Seasoning is ready to be used.*

CHAPTER NINETEEN

NAVARATNA MILLETS

A royal taste of millets cooked in a healthy style to satiate your taste buds with goodness of health for a happy tummy!!!

Ingredients

- Millets – 2 Cup, pre-cooked
- Chopped Vegetables – 1 Cup (cauliflower, carrot, green peas, french beans)
- Paneer - ½ cup diced
- Chopped Coriander Leaves – 1 tablespoon
- Chopped Mint Leaves – 1 tablespoon
- Onions - ½ cup chopped
- Ginger and Garlic Paste - 1 tablespoon
- Curd - 3 tablespoon
- Lime Juice - 1 tablespoon
- Green Chillies– 2 slitted
- Dry Fruits - Cashews, Almonds and Raisins - ½ cup
- Shah Jeera – ½ tablespoon
- Dalchini (Cinnamon) - 1 Inch stick
- Tej patta (Bay Leaves) - 2
- Black Pepper - 8 to 10
- Magic Spice Mix - 1 tablespoon
- Ghee / Oil – 3 tablespoons
- Turmeric powder - ½ tablespoon
- Salt – ½ tablespoon or as per taste

Procedure

- Take a Kadhai or a Pan and put it on medium heat. Add Ghee/oil and let it heat. Add the dry fruits and fry them golden brown. Once done, take them out and keep it aside. Add Shah Jeera, onions and all the whole spices, sauté for 1-2 minutes. Add ginger-garlic paste and stir for 20-30 seconds. Add coriander and mint leaves and fry them for 1-2 minutes. Add the chopped vegetables, paneer, salt to taste and Magic Spice Mix. Stir for 3-4 minutes till the vegetables are done. Add the curd now and stir for another 2-3 minutes. Add the pre-cooked millets, lime juice, green chillies and slowly mix them well and stir them for 2-3 minutes. Add the fried dry fruits and mix them well. Switch off the heat and cover the pan for 1-2 minutes before serving.
- Serve hot with any of the side dishes. (Recipe #18)

CHAPTER TWENTY

REFRESHING DRINK'S

For a refreshing experience!!!

Ginger-Lime Drink

Ingredients

- Water - ½ litre or 500ml
- Jaggery (Gud) – 5 tablespoons
- Lemon Juice – 1 Lemon
- Crushed Ginger - 1 Inch piece
- Rock Salt - ½ tablespoon

Procedure

Pour all the ingredients in a deep bowl and keep them aside for 15-20 minutes. Mix them well and strain the drink. Serve for a refreshing experience.

Cucumber-Mint-Lime Drink

Ingredients

- Water - ½ litre or 500ml
- Jaggery (Gud) – 5 tablespoons
- Lemon Juice – 1 Lemon
- Grated Cucumber - 3 tablespoons
- Mint leaves - 8-10 leaves
- Rock Salt - ½ tablespoon

Procedure

Pour all the ingredients in a deep bowl and keep them aside for 15-20 minutes. Crush the mint leaves and add to the water. Mix them well and strain the drink. Serve for a refreshing experience.

CHAPTER TWENTY-ONE

QUICK COOKING TIPS

*You can **wash and soak the millets** for 10 minutes. Soaked millets can be used in any of the recipes mentioned in this book. Add the water proportion (1 cup millets need 2 cups luke warm water) and then simmer with a closed lid, till the millets are done.*

*When using the pre-cooked millets, always **cover the pan for 2-3 minutes** after removing from the heat or before serving. This allows the millets to soak the complete flavour of the dish.*

*Always cook in **medium heat** to retain the flavour of the spices and goodness of the ingredients used.*

***Balance the salt** as per your taste.*

***Desi ghee** is always preferred over any refined oil.*

Pre-cut all the vegetables like carrot, cabbage, beans, cauliflower and store them in the refrigerator in airtight boxes for reducing cooking time. This can be stored for a week. Do not wash them while cutting, while using for any dishes, then wash.

Prepare **ginger-garlic paste and add a little salt** to it. Store in refrigerator in airtight box. This can be stored for a week.

Use **Jaggery (Gud)** for adding sweetness instead of sugar. Jaggery has rich source of iron, minerals and fibre along with calories. It should be consumed in moderation.

Use luke warm water while cooking for any of the dishes. This helps to cook faster and removes the raw water smell from the dishes.